Pradheep Manisekaran

A Novel Approach To Enhance The Performance Of Cloud Computing File System Using Load Balancing Algorithm

A Model To Enhance The Performance Of Cloud Computing File System Using Round Robin Algorithm

GRIN Publishing

Bibliographic information published by the German National Library:

The German National Library lists this publication in the National Bibliography; detailed bibliographic data are available on the Internet at http://dnb.dnb.de .

Imprint:

Copyright © 2014 GRIN Verlag GmbH
Print and binding: Books on Demand GmbH, Norderstedt Germany
ISBN: 978-3-656-89042-3

This book at GRIN:

http://www.grin.com/en/e-book/288801/a-novel-approach-to-enhance-the-perfor-mance-of-cloud-computing-file-system

GRIN - Your knowledge has value

Since its foundation in 1998, GRIN has specialized in publishing academic texts by students, college teachers and other academics as e-book and printed book. The website www.grin.com is an ideal platform for presenting term papers, final papers, scientific essays, dissertations and specialist books.

Visit us on the internet:

Http://www.grin.com/

Http://www.facebook.com/grincom

Http://www.twitter.com/grin_com

CHAPTER 1 - INTRODUCTION

Introduction Of Cloud Computing: Cloud Computing is one of the largest technology enhancement in recent times. It has taken computing in initial to the next level. Cloud computing is one of the biggest thing in computing in current time. Cloud computing is a wide elucidation that provides IT as a service. Cloud computing uses the internet and the central remote servers to support different data and applications. It is an internet based technology. It permits the users to approach their personal files at any computer with internet access [9]. The cloud computing suppleness is a function of the allocation of resources on authority's request. Cloud computing provides the act of uniting. Cloud computing is that emerging technology which is used for providing various computing and storage services by means the Internet [1]. In the cloud computing, the internet is viewed as a cloud. By the use of cloud computing, the capital and operational costs can be cut.

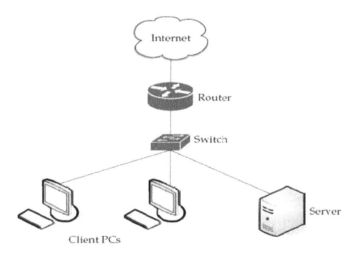

Fig 1.1: A cloud is used in network diagrams to depict the Internet

Cloud computing incorporates the various features such as infrastructure, platform, and software as services. These service providers rent based data center hardware and software to deliver storage and computing services through the Internet. Internet users can obtain services from a cloud as if they were employing a super computer which be using cloud computing. Storing data in the cloud is an alternative of on their own devices and it making everywhere data access possible and can access it at any place and time by using internet. They can run their applications on much more influential cloud computing platforms come with software services in the cloud which reduces the users work load of software installation and frequent upgrade on their end local devices.

1.1 Major Trends In Cloud Computing:
Cloud computing has exponential growth over the last few years. Few of the major current trends in the industry today are follows.

- **Hybrid clouds:**

Hybrid clouds are the combination of both public and private clouds. The information technology executives gets the more choices for personalized solutions while big data advocates and security experts are still satisfied. The hybrid models become the main stream [23].

- **BYOD(Bring Your Own Device):**

Now a day, BYOD comes into picture. End users are using their own various kinds of mobile devices to put more and more of their own data into personal cloud services for storage the file system. The information technology departments use to integrates the personal cloud services to help other employees. In the BYOD many tools are required as: Mobile device management.

- **Platform-as-a-Service (PaaS)**:

Platform as a service enables the businesses to reduce their Information technology costs. These applications are increasing their development efficiently through effective testing and development methods.

- **Web-powered apps:**

Cloud computing is a web based application. Data efficiency and scalability are the primary benefits of cloud computing. The cloud based applications are develop according to their compatibility with multiple platforms

3

Fig 1.2 : Cloud Synchronization

- **Big data analytics:**

This phase is similar to the public and private cloud model. Now days many organizations combines the big data analytics with the cloud computing. They don't choose the one file than next. This service offers the big data analysis. Its size is attainable and scalable.

- **Graphics as a service:**

To run high level graphical applications on hardware, very high quality hardware is required for that. For this purpose, we need a very large investment. With the help of Cloud computing it is very easy to run these applications on this platform. There are many new technologies in the cloud computing that helps to increase the cloud-based graphics technologies from prominent graphics companies.

- **Identity management and protection:**

In the cloud computing, security is the big issue. Now a day, everyone stores data into the cloud. Every time a person stores his/her information on cloud, the data in the cloud increasing rapidly. Hence any person can access the data from cloud database. Hence the data save in the cloud is not secure. There are many methods to enhance the security in the database.

4

1.2 Key Features Of Cloud Computing:

Cloud computing is an emerging new technology. Cloud computing is associated with the cost beneficial system. Here security and privacy is the main concern.[24]

- **Use of Resources**

In the cloud computing many resources are used. These resources are pooled together. These resources are used to serve large number of customers. Cloud computer uses the many applications. One of the main applications is multi-tenancy. In this case, different resources are dynamically allocated and de-allocated according to the demand of the customer. In the user end, it is very difficult to know that where resources are reside actually. The allocation of the resources should be elastic. The elasticity of resources helps in allocate the resources on demand.

- **Self-Service and On-demand Services**

Cloud computing is works basically on this two models. These model are self service and on demand **service models**. It allows many users to interact with the cloud. The cloud performs many tasks like, building, deploying, managing, and scheduling. The user can access many computing abilities, when they are required. They do not require any interaction with cloud-service provider. This would help users to be in control, bringing agility in their work.

- **Pricing**

Cloud computing does not have any upfront cost. The cost of the cloud computing is based upon its usage. The user need to pay the bill based on the amount of resources they are using. It will provide the tracking services to the user. Hence user can increase or reduce their cost on the basis of resource utilization. In the cloud computing, the information gather should be crystal clear and offered to the customer. It is very much necessary to make the customer recognize the cost profit that cloud computing brings.

- **Quality of Service**

Cloud computing be required to guarantee the best service level for users. it should have high availability. There are many services that a cloud system provides; it includes round-the-clock availability, adequate resources, performance, and bandwidth. Any compromise on these guarantees could prove fatal for customers.

1.3 The Essential Characteristics of Cloud Computing

Cloud computing is used for large and small organizations. Here are the main characteristics that cloud computing offers businesses today.

- **On-demand capabilities:**

In the cloud computing, business is the secure cloud hosting service. The user can easily access these services directly or with the help of service provider. User can also change these services according to their need. User can add or delete users and change storage networks and software as wanted.

- **Broad network access:**

If we are working in a tram, it provides the service called, broad network access. In this case, the team can access the various business management issues in the cloud by using laptops, smart-phones etc. In a team, an online access point is available for each team member. The users can use these kinds of devices wherever they want they just need to position with a simple online access point. Broad network right of entry includes private clouds that run within a company's firewall, public clouds, or a hybrid deployment.

- **Resource pooling:**

Cloud computer enable many services for the user. An employee can store or access data at the same time and from the any location [22].

- **Measured service:**

In this case, Use and Pay service is available. Here the services we can use, we have to pay for them only. No extra payment is there. Hence the total amount of resources a user use and control, only that much amount he/she has to pay.

1.4 Components Of Cloud Computing:

Cloud computing consists of three main components. These components are:

- Clients
- Datacenter
- Distributed servers.

Each element in cloud computing plays a specific role.

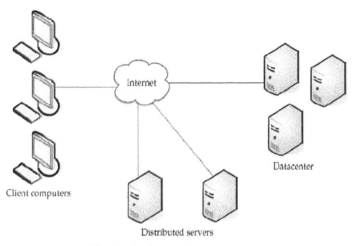

Fig 1.3: cloud computing components

- **Clients**

In the cloud computing, the information is managed by end users. End users can interact with the clients to manage information that is related to clouds. The clients are further organize into three categories[7]:

- ➤ **Mobile Client:** the clients can be mobile in nature. It includes windows mobile smart phone, like a Blackberry or I Phone.
- ➤ **Thin:** These clients do not do computation work. They only used to display information. These clients don't have the internal memory; the servers do all the work for the clients.
- ➤ **Thick:** These clients use different browsers to connect the internet cloud. And they have storage devices and processing features. Through browsers such as internet explorer, Mozilla Firefox or Google Chrome connected with the Internet cloud.

- **Datacenter**

Datacenter is a group of servers; these servers host the various applications. The end users connect to the datacenter. Datacenter is existing at very large distance from the clients.

- **Distributed Servers**

Distributed servers are the part of a cloud computing, these servers are present all through the Internet. These sever hosts the various applications.

7

1.5 Virtualization:

The clouds are of three types: Public Clouds, Private Clouds and the Hybrid Clouds. Virtualization is one of the useful and high featured concept in context of cloud systems. Virtualization means something that is not real. Virtualization is a software implementation of computer. It helps to perform special programs like a real machine. It is related to cloud computing because virtualization can be used by end users and the end users use the different services of a cloud. The types of virtualization are originated in case of clouds as given in [7]:

- Full virtualization
- Partial virtualization

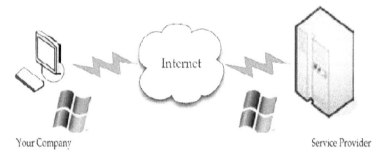

Your Company   Service Provider

Fig 1.4: Full virtualization

- **Full Virtualization**

In case of full virtualization, we can create an environment like our real system. But in this case, we have to completely install these applications on the virtual machine. The full virtualization is used for [7]:

  o Sharing a computer system among different users
  o It helps to Isolates users from each additional and from the control program
  o Emulating hardware on an additional machine

- **Partial virtualization**

In partial virtualization, the hardware allows different operating systems simultaneously to run on single machine by well-organized use of system resources such as memory and

8

processor. In this case, the services are not fully available. These services are provided partially at the need of it. It has the following advantages:

- **Disaster recovery:** It helps in the disaster recovery.
- **Migration:** in the virtualization, hardware can be replaced easily, hence migration of dissimilar parts of a new machine is faster.
- **Capacity management:** here we can manage the capacity according to the need of customer. It is an easier and faster way to change or replace the applications.

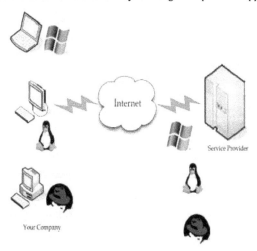

Fig 1.5: Partial virtualization

1.6 Features of cloud computing

- **Scalability**

Cloud computing has high scalability. This means we can extend our usability at whatever time we need some more additional resources we can included it to the cloud anytime. Generally Cloud computing is endless pool of resources.

- **Environment friendly**

Cloud computing utilize the hardware in very good efficient manner h so that it helps to reduce energy price.

- **Cost efficient**

Most important characteristic and advantage of cloud computing is, it is cost efficient. The user needs to pay only for the amount which they used just like electricity bill.

- **Up to date**

We should not to worry about the frequent updating process of software's and hardware's that we are using in the cloud. The supplier is in charge for the overall update process of all the components [8].

- **Improved performance**

Whenever we need to extend some more additional features and high configuration resources it can be available to the user on basis of demand [8].

1.7 Cloud Computing Architecture

Cloud computing system is divides into two sections:

- Front end

- Back end.

The systems connected with each other through the internet. The front end is the side of computer user. In the front end side, all the application and platform will be presents that are compulsory to access cloud computing system. The back end is the cloud section of the system. In the back end system, various computers, servers and data storage systems are present that performs the computing storage and data sharing operations.[15]. In the cloud computing, each function has its own server. The central server help in administers the system, monitoring traffic and client demands. It follows a set of rules, generally known as the protocols. These protocols used a extraordinary kind of software called middleware.

Middleware allows the network computers to communicate with each other. In this case, the time servers don't run with full capability. Hence it is possible to fool a physical server and it also looks like a single system .The physical server may think that there are multiple servers and each running with its own independent operating system. This technique is known as server virtualization. By using the output of individual servers, it reduces the need for more physical machines.

Cloud computing systems have to at least double the number of storage devices it requires to keep all its clients information stored. A cloud computing system generally makes copies of all its clients information and store it on additional devices so that at time of data loss it can be utilized.[15]

1.8 Cloud Computing Applications

The applications of cloud computing are immeasurable. By the use of right middleware, a cloud computing system could execute all the programs a ordinary computer could run. There are some basic applications of cloud computing:

- In the cloud computing, clients can easily access the applications and data from cloud at any time. The cloud can be access by using computer system that is connected to the internet.
- Cloud computing systems can decrease the need for superior hardware on the client side. There is no need to buy a faster computer with large memory,[9] because the cloud system would take care of those needs for you.
- Cloud computing systems give the access to computer application for many organizations. The companies do not buy the particular set of software and the software licenses for each employee.
- In the cloud computing, servers and digital storage devices take up space.

1.9 Load Balancing
It is a method of reassigning the total load to the individual nodes of the collective system. Load balancing helps to make resource utilization effective and also used to improve the response time of the job. The load balancing helps to remove the nodes which are unbalanced. In this situation it removes the nodes, which are overloaded or under loaded. It is active in nature. It does not consider the previous [3] behavior of system. While developing this algorithm, some factors are come into picture, as:
- Estimation of load
- Comparison of load
- Stability of different system
- Performance of system
- Interaction between the nodes
- Nature of work to be transferred
- Selecting of nodes.

11

1.10 Goals of Load balancing:

The goals of load balancing are:

- Helps to get better the performance substantially
- It have a backup plan in case the system fails even partially
- Used to maintain the system stability
- Helps to accommodate potential modification in the system

1.11 Types of Load balancing algorithms:

The load balancing algorithms are classified into the three categories [3]:

- **Sender Initiated:** In this case the load balancing algorithm is initialized by the sender.
- **Receiver Initiated**: Here the load balancing algorithm is initiated by the receiver.
- **Symmetric Initiated**: It is the mixture of both sender initiated and receiver initiated

Depending on the present state of the system, load balancing algorithms can be alienated into two categories [2]:

- **Static:** It does not depend on the present state of the system. In this case the prior knowledge of the system is required.
- **Dynamic:** Decisions on load balancing are based on recent state of the system. No prior information is needed. So it is better than static approach.

Dynamic Load balancing algorithm

In a distributed system, dynamic load balancing can be done in two different ways:

- Distributed
- Non distributed.

In the distributed dynamic load balancing algorithm, the load balancing is executed by all nodes present in the system and the task of load balancing is shared among them.

1.12 File System in cloud computing:

Now days, the growth of communication and the technologies have transformed the way we live and work. The cloud computing is an up-and-coming technology. In the cloud computing storage area is used. For storing the information in storage area various files are required. To maintain these files file systems are used. These files systems include:

- **Hadoop Distributed File System:** these file systems deploys in large scale distributed system. These file system includes facebook, google, yahoo and so on. These file systems use a name node to maintain a directory of all files in the cloud and their respective metadata. In this the name node has to manage all the files related operations, these files related operation includes open, copy, move, delete, update, etc.

- **Network File System:** It is a way to carve up files between different machines on a network. These files are positioned on the client local hard drive. One of the disadvantages of NFS is that it tries to make a remote file system that appears as a local file system.

- **Andrew File System:** It is a distributed networked system, which uses a set of trusted servers to present a homogeneous, location transparent file name space to all the client workstations. AFS uses Kerberos for authentication and implements access control lists on directories for users and groups.

- **Blue Sky File System:** The blue sky film system uses the object data structures maintained in the file system. And their association in a log-structured format. The Blue Sky file systems use to clean the logs comprising file system. Blue Sky uses four types of objects for on behalf of data and metadata in its log structured file system format:

  ➤ Data blocks
  ➤ I nodes
  ➤ I node maps
  ➤ Checkpoints

Blue Sky does not use indirect blocks for locating file data. I nodes directly contain pointers to all the data blocks.

- **Lustre File System**

  It is a scalable parallel distributed file system. It is capable of handling large amount of storage with extremely high aggregate throughput. A Lustre installation comprises three types of systems:

  o The clients that request file system services
  o Object Storage Servers

     o   Object Storage Targets

- **Mirror File System**

MFS has two exclusive features that allow it to offer benefits for Cloud Computing both the users and service providers. Replication at the File System Software Module Level allows file replication among two separate systems in true time. same data will be stored and maintained in two different places .A user can have two copies of the similar file on two systems, one on the local desktop, the other one on the Cloud server. This helps to in the case of data crash and in the absence of availability .it creates transition or relocation from local computing to Cloud Computing simple and faultless. For the service provider, copies of the identical file can be simulated in multiple data centers in real time, which helps to create the process of the Cloud service very well-organized and always obtainable. MFS does not check the storage systems to be communal and confined physically to one data center, the service providers can scale the operation up from one data center to multiple data centers easily as needed and vice the security algorithms. Each data center has its individual system and its own storage, but contains information the same to that of the other data centers. The distributed capability of MFS makes the Cloud Computing service much more reliable and efficient.

1.13 Round Robin Algorithm:

Round robin algorithm is a simplest and most widely used scheduling algorithm. It is used for the time sharing systems. The small unit of time is known as quantum. In the round robin algorithm, all the run-able process is kept in a queue. The CPU scheduler allots a quantum of time to each processor. At each quantum the processor performs their task. The new processes are added on its tail. [22] The CPU scheduler picks the first process from the queue, sets a timer to interrupt after one quantum, and dispatches the process. If the process is still running at the end of the quantum, the CPU is preempted and the process is added to the tail of the queue. If the process finishes before the end of the quantum, the process itself releases the CPU. The round-robin scheduling algorithm is designed for time-sharing systems. It is similar to first come first serve scheduling. A time quantum is generally from 10 to 100 milliseconds.

To implement RR scheduling:

- Ready queue as a FIFO queue of processes.
- New processes are added to the tail of the ready queue.[22]
- The CPU scheduler picks the first process from the ready queue, sets a timer to interrupt after 1 time quantum, and dispatches the process.
- The process may have a CPU burst of less than 1 time quantum.

.The CPU scheduler will then select the next process in the ready queue.

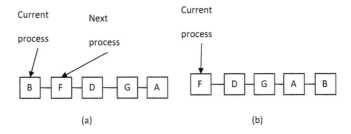

(a)   (b)

Fig 1.6: Round-robin scheduling. (a) The list of runnable processes. (b) The list of runnable processes after B uses up its quantum.

- The average waiting time under the RR policy is often long. Consider the following set of processes that arrive at time 0, with the length of the CPU burst given in milliseconds:

	Burst	Waiting	Turnaround
Process	Time	Time	Time
P_1	24	6	30
P_2	3	4	7
P_3	3	7	10
Average	-	5.66	15.66

Fig 1.7: Processes

Using round-robin scheduling, we would schedule these processes according to the following chart:

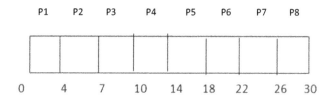

Fig 1.8: Scheduling Processes

- In the RR scheduling algorithm, no process is allocated the CPU for more than 1 time quantum in a row.
- If a process's CPU burst exceeds 1 time quantum, that process is preempted and is put back in the ready queue. The RR scheduling algorithm is thus pre-emptive.

16

- o If there are n processes in the ready queue and the time quantum is q, then each process gets $\frac{1}{n}$ of the CPU time in chunks of at most q time units.

- o Each process must wait no longer than $\underline{\hspace{1cm}(n-1)*q\hspace{1cm}}$ time units until its next time quantum.

- The performance of the RR algorithm depends heavily on the size of the time quantum.

  - o If the time quantum is extremely large, the RR policy is the same as the FCFS policy.
  - o If the time quantum is extremely small (say, 1 millisecond), the RR approach is called processor sharing and (in theory) creates the appearance that each of n processes has its own processor running at $\frac{1}{n}$ the speed of the real processor.

- We need also to consider the effect of context switching on the performance of RR scheduling. Switching from one process to another requires a certain amount of time for doing the administration saving and loading registers and memory maps, updating various tables and lists, flushing and reloading the memory cache, etc.

  - o Let us assume that we have only one process of 10 time units.
  - o If the quantum is 12 time units, the process finishes in less than 1 time quantum, with no overhead.
  - o If the quantum is 6 time units, however, the process requires 2 quanta, resulting in a context switch.
  - o If the time quantum is 1 time unit, then nine context switches will occur, slowing the execution of the process accordingly

- Thus, we want the time quantum to be large with respect to the context-switch time.

- Setting the quantum too short causes too many process switches and lowers the CPU efficiency, but setting it too long may cause poor response to short interactive requests.

- Poor average waiting time when job lengths are identical; Imagine 10 jobs each requiring 10 time slices, all complete after about 100 time slices, even FCFS is better!

- In general, the average turnaround time can be improved if most processes finish their next CPU burst in a single time quantum. If context-switch time is added in, the average turnaround time increases for a smaller time quantum, since more context switches are required.

- Although the time quantum should be large compared with the context-switch time, it should not be too large. If the time quantum is too large, RR scheduling degenerates to FCFS policy.

CHAPTER 2 - LITERATURE SURVEY

Tejinder Sharma, et.al, (2013): in this paper author discuss concerning the cloud computing. As, the computer networks are still in their infancy, however they rise up and become complicated. Cloud computing is rising as a fresh paradigm of enormous scale distributed computing. It changes of concept of storing of data. It makes us to move computing and data away from local systems desktop and portable PCs, into giant data centers. it has the potential to harness the facility of internet and wide area network to use resources that are available remotely.[11] There are several security problems in the cloud computing. In this paper, author discuss regarding the various scheduling problems. One of the difficult scheduling issues in Cloud datacenters is to take the allocation and migration of reconfigurable virtual machines into deliberation moreover as the integrated features of hosting physical machines. In order to pick out the virtual nodes for executing the task, Load equalization is a methodology to distribute workload across multiple computers. The major purpose of this paper to recommend well-organized and enhanced scheduling algorithm that can maintain the load equalization and provides better improved strategies through efficient job scheduling and customized resource allocation techniques. One of the difficult scheduling issues in Cloud datacenters is to take the allocation and relocation of reconfigurable virtual machines into consideration as well as the integrated features of hosting physical machines. In order to pick out the virtual nodes for executing the task, Load equalization is a methodology to distribute workload across multiple computers, or other resources over the network links to achieve most favorable resource utilization, minimum data processing time, smallest amount average reply time, and keep away from overload.

Sonal Guleria, Dr. Sonia Vatta, (2013): describes that the Cloud computing is emerging field owing to its performance, high availability, least price and plenty of others. In cloud computing, the data are going to be stored in storage provided by service suppliers. Cloud computing provides a computer user right of entry to information Technology (IT) services that contains applications, servers, data storage, without requiring an considerate of the technology. An analogy to an electricity computing grid is to be helpful for cloud computing. To enabling convenient and on-demand network access to a shared pool of configurable computing resources are used for as a model of cloud computing.[21] Cloud computing will be expressed as a mix of Software-as-a-Service that refers to a service release model to enabling used for business services of software interface and can be combined making new business services delivered via flexible networks and Platform as a Service Cloud systems giving an extra abstraction level which activity a virtualized infrastructure that can offer the software platform where systems should be run on and Infrastructure as a Service which suppliers manage an outsized set of computing resources which is used for storing and processing capacity. However still several business corporations are not willing to adopt cloud computing technology owing to lack of proper security management policy and weakness in safeguard that result in several vulnerability in cloud computing. This paper has been written to focus on the matter of data security. to confirm the safety of users' information within the cloud, we tend to propose an efficient and flexible theme with two different algorithms .A user can access cloud services as a utility service and begin to use them almost right away. These features that create cloud computing so flexible with the very fact that services are accessible wherever any time result in more than a few potential risks. The key intent of this analysis work is to study the existing security schemes and to verify information privacy, integrity and authentication.

Amandeep Kaur Sidhu, Supriya Kinger, (2013): discuss concerning the various load balancing algorithms in cloud computing. Cloud Computing is a rising computing model. Its aim is to share data, calculations, and service clearly over a scalable network of nodes. Cloud computing stores the data and disseminated resources within the open atmosphere. Cloud Computing could be a framework for enabling a suitable, on-demand network access to a shared pool of computing resources. These resources are often provisioned and de-provisioned. Owing to the exponential growth of cloud computing, it has been wide adopted by the business and there is a fast improvement in data centers [4]. Within the cloud storage, load balancing could be a key issue. It might consume lots of price to take care of load data, since the system is just too huge to timely disperse load. Load balancing is of the main challenges in cloud computing that is wanted to distribute the dynamic work across multiple nodes to make sure that no single node is besieged.

Satoshi Togawa et.al, (2013): explains in this paper about the private cloud that is used for the disaster recovery. In this paper, [19] author built a framework of disaster recovery. Here author build a model system that is supported IaaS architecture. The model system is built by several private cloud computing fabrics. In this case, distributed storage system is used to build a personal cloud fabric. The distributed storage system is used to handle the massive file systems. The distributed storage systems are ready to keep running as one large filing system when some private cloud fabric does not work by any troubles. In this paper the author show repose cloud cooperation framework.

Hung-Chang Hsiao, Hsueh-Yi Chung, Haiying Shen, and Yu-Chang Chao (2013): In this paper, author discuss about the load rebalancing for distributed file systems in clouds. Cloud computing is a compelling technology. In clouds, the clients are dynamically allocated to their resources on-demand without sophisticated deployment and management of resources.

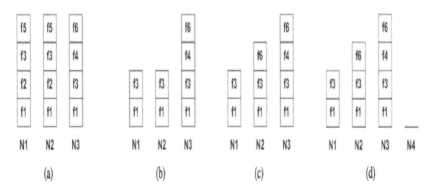

Fig 2.1: File chunks in cloud computing

Distributed file systems are major key factor for cloud computing applications based on the Map Reduce programming paradigm [17].In these file systems, nodes are simultaneously serve computing and storage functions. In distributed file system, the load of a node is relative to the number of file chunks the node possesses. In distributed files system, file can also be dynamically created, deleted, and appended. This results in load imbalance in a distributed file system. In this paper, author use a algorithm and compare this algorithm against a centralized approach in a production system and a competing distributed solution.

21

Jasmin James, et.al, (2012): Discuss regarding the security in cloud computing. Cloud computing is quick growing area in computing analysis. With the advancement of the Cloud, several new prospects are coming into picture, like however applications is engineered and the way completely different services is offered to the end user through Virtualization. There are the cloud services providers who give giant scaled computing infrastructure outlined on usage, and provide the infrastructure services in a very versatile manner. The virtualization forms the foundation of cloud technology wherever [12] Virtualization is a rising IT paradigm that separates computing functions and technology implementations from physical hardware. By using virtualization, users will access servers while not knowing specific server details. The virtualization layer can execute user request for computing resources by accessing acceptable resources. in this paper, author foremost analyses the various Virtual Machine (VM) load balancing algorithms. Secondly, a brand new VM load balancing algorithmic rule has been proposed and enforced for an IaaS framework in simulated cloud computing environment.

Abhisek Pan, John Paul Walters (2012): In this paper, author integrates the high performance file systems in a cloud computing environment. The flexibility, scalability, and dynamic provisioning capabilities provided by a cloud computing infrastructure make it an attractive platform for running high performance computing applications [17]. In order to attain acceptable HPC performance in a cloud environment, the applications running in virtual machine instances must have access to a high performance file system. The absence of a dedicated file system service in the cloud means that virtual parallel file systems have to be deployed inside virtual machine. In this paper, author uses ongoing efforts to effectively integrate a parallel file system in a cloud environment. They investigate how a parallel file system can be effectively integrated and provided as a service to cloud users running High Performance Computing (HPC) applications

Luyang Dong and Bin Gong et al (2011): In this paper a tree scheduling strategy is used for the development of large scale computing system resource allocation is done in dynamic environment where multiple jobs are executed [10]. A scenario is made in which the job passes from the main scheduler to the system scheduler and from the system scheduler to the nodes from where the jobs are allocated to the processors. A proposed policy is used which improved the adaptive hierarchical scheduling and performance enhancement in the targets to develop such a system which can execute number of jobs

22

on multiple processors which can take less time and work more efficiently as compared to existing systems in secured environment. Various approaches are used like the space sharing and time sharing. It helps to balance the load of number of jobs on processors and also helps to allocate that job the processor can execute according to its capacity which results in getting less wait time for the jobs. The space sharing technique also allows splitting the job on different processors if one processor is not able to fulfill the requirements of the job then the job will be split on the different processors which makes job to be executed in less time. The proposed system also uses the demand driven approach to make the results of the system more efficient.

Jaliya Ekanayake and Geoffrey Fox (2010): in this paper, author discuss concerning the high performance parallel computing with clouds and cloud technologies. The provisioning of resources happens in minutes as against the hours and days needed within the case of ancient queue-based job scheduling systems.[14] the utilization of such virtualized resources permits the user to fully customize the Virtual Machine (VM) images and use them with root/administrative privileges, that is another feature that is laborious to realize with traditional infrastructures. Infrastructure services provided by cloud vendors permit any user to provision an oversized range of compute instances fairly simply. Among several parallelizable issues, most parallel applications can be performed using MapReduce technologies like Hadoop, CGL-MapReduce, and Dryad, in a very fairly simple manner. There are several scientific applications that have advanced communication pattern. These patterns need low latency communication mechanisms and rich set of communication constructs offered by runtime.

Debessay Fesehaye, Rahul malik, Klara Nahrstedt (2010): in this paper, author discuss regarding distributed file system in cloud computing. The communication technologies remodeled the manner we tend to live and work. The communication technologies have the potential to rework an outsized a part of the IT business. a number of the challenge embrace data transfer bottlenecks, performance unpredictability, scalable storage, quick scaling to variable workloads, etc. managing these challenges of enormous scale distributed data, compute and storage intensive applications like social networks and search engines needs robust, scalable and economical algorithms and protocols [5].The Google file system and Hadoop Distributed file system are the leading general algorithms deployed in giant scale distributed systems like Facebook, Google and Yahoo nowadays.

23

In this paper, author addresses these issues with current systems like the GFS/HDFS. So as to form the system scalable, this scheme uses a light weight front-end server to attach all requests with several name nodes. This helps distribute load of one name node to several name nodes. To beat these issues of HDFS we tend to present a brand new distributed file system. Our scheme uses a light weight front server to attach all requests with several name nodes.

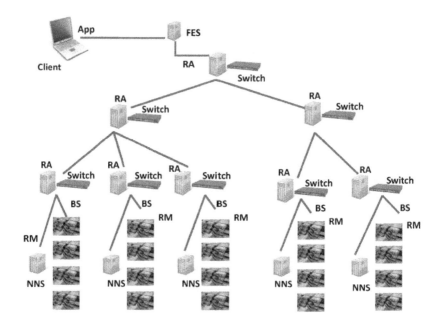

Fig 2.2: Working of paper

Cong Wang, Qian Wang, (2010): in this paper, author discuss concerning the data storage security in cloud computing. Cloud Computing has been visualized because the next generation design of IT enterprise. As a turbulent technology with profound implications, Cloud Computing is remodeling the terribly nature of however businesses use info technology. One elementary aspect of this paradigm shifting is that data is being centralized or outsourced into the Cloud. From users perspective, as well as each individuals and IT enterprises, storing data remotely into the cloud in a very versatile on-demand manner brings appealing advantages [18]. Cloud computing is that the long unreal vision of computing as a utility, wherever users will remotely store their data into the cloud thus on get pleasure from the on-demand prime quality applications and services from a shared pool of configurable computing resources. By data outsourcing, users may be relieved from the burden of local data storage and maintenance. To securely introduce a good third party auditor (TPA), the subsequent 2 fundamental necessities have to be compelled to be met: 1) TPA ought to be able to expeditiously audit the cloud data storage while not stern the local copy of data, and introduce no extra on-line burden to the cloud user; 2) The third party auditing method ought to usher in no new vulnerabilities towards user data privacy. in this paper, author utilize and unambiguously combine the general public key based mostly similarity authenticator with random masking to realize the privacy-preserving public cloud data auditing system, that meets all higher than necessities.

J. H. Abawajy et al. (2009) had given the concept of multiple resources distributed geographically. Optimization is the most critical area in cloud computing environments. Resource allocation and time scheduling are an area that needs to be taken under high consideration especially if our motive of improvement is performance enhancement [13]. For many jobs, I/O is an exploring resource. Most of the data from the grid are going to be an online system. The assignment of resources and the processor must be synchronized for the efficient performance. For this tree scheduling policy is used to accommodate parallel jobs to manage the background workload. A static space time splitting strategy is put in place to estimate the planned performance. Diverse issues in large multiprocessor system are posed by the main scheduler. The parallel processing system has been merged into the grid and cluster computing system. The sharing of large no of computers by a variety of users causes a major problem in the allocation of resources and the proper allocation of the tasks. Selecting a scheduling algorithm that is not fit will lead to the bad performance of the system and the utilization. A service provider makes computing resources available to the customer, as required, and charges them for specific use rather than charge a flat rate. The resource allocation and scheduling are addressed. A Vertical framework is used that defines power b/w data and resources in an enterprise grid computing system.

CHAPTER 3 - PRESENT WORK

3. Present Work:

Cloud computing use the computing, platform, software as a service. Cloud Computing refers to the use of computing, platform, software, as a service. It's a form of utility computing where the customer needs not to own the entire thing instead of that the user can select necessary infrastructure and pay only for what they used. Computing resources are delivered as virtual machines. And all the storage is done by distributes file systems. In such a scenario, task scheduling and load balancing algorithms in file system play a vital role in scheduling the tasks effectively, and to store, process and share the data effectively. So that to reduce the turnaround time and improve resource utilization. This paper presents a load balancing based Round robin algorithms for scheduling tasks in cloud computing file system in the consideration of computational complexity and computing capacity of processing elements. In another hand it is very important to safeguard the security of data present in file system so in our work some additional techniques have been added to provide security for the data. Experimental results show that proposed algorithms exhibit good performance under heavy loads. Thus our main goal is to enhance the performance of file system in cost wise and security wise. Cloud computing is a high performance computing environment with a large scale, heterogeneous collection of autonomous systems and flexible computational architecture. To improve the overall performance of cloud computing, with the deadline constraint, a task scheduling model is established for reducing the system power consumption of cloud computing and improving the profit of service providers. For the scheduling model, a solving method based on multi-objective genetic algorithm is designed and the research is focused on encoding rules, crossover operators, selection operators and the method of sorting Pareto solutions.

3.1 Problem Formulation:

Large scale distributed systems such as cloud computing applications are getting very general. These applications come with lot of new challenges and issues in transferring, storing and computing data. At present much kind of challenges in distributed file systems is dealing by Hadoop file system (HDFS) and Google file system (GFS). But HDFS has some major issues. The most important factor is that it depends on one name node to handle the majority operations of every data block in the file system. As a result it may be result in a bottleneck resource and one purpose of failure. The second potential problem which is present in HDFS is that it totally depends on the help of TCP to transfer data. Usually TCP takes several rounds to process and it consumes lot of time before it will send at the complete capability of the links in the cloud. This results in low link utilization and longer downloads times. In such case, nodes concurrently serve computing and storage functions; a file is divided into a number of chunks allocated in distinct nodes so to perform parallel process over the nodes MapReduce tasks will be performed. However, in a cloud computing process, failures are most common thing due to its huge architecture, and nodes could also be upgraded, replaced, and added in the system. Files can even be dynamically created, deleted, and appended. This results in load imbalance in a distributed file system; that's, the file chunks aren't distributed as uniformly as potential among the nodes so that data loss and time delay may occur. Growing distributed file systems in production systems fully based on a central node for chunk reallocation. This confidence is clearly insufficient in a large-scale, failure-prone setting as a result of the central load balancer is put out vital workload that's linearly scaled with the system size, and should therefore become the performance bottleneck and therefore the single purpose of failure. Suppose we tend to save the files in cloud and a few third party accesses those files and add some extraneous information which will damage our system. thus to boost the performance and security of cloud computing in this thesis we use a new approach called load balancing with round robin algorithm.

3.2 Objectives:
The objectives of the work are as following:

- Use round robin to schedule jobs for file system load balancing in cloud computing.
- To enhance the performance of file system.
- To enhance the security level of file system
- To schedule more number of jobs in less time.
- To decrease time to process jobs and cost of transaction
- To remove the deadlocks and server overflow

3.3 Methodology:

Load Balancing: child node distributed the equal number of jobs. job schedules on process to find the efficiency by using the round robin algorithm it gives the response time in the next step balance the load it's also called a space sharing. In hierarchy of scheduling of algorithm there is a one light weight main server. The main server contains number of main sub systems and the main sub systems contain further sub system at level 2 as shown in figure. Now at level 2 each sub system is having 8 nodes . Now we have 9 nodes at LEVEL 2 and each system contain further 8 more nodes so now here we are having 9*8 =72 child nodes.

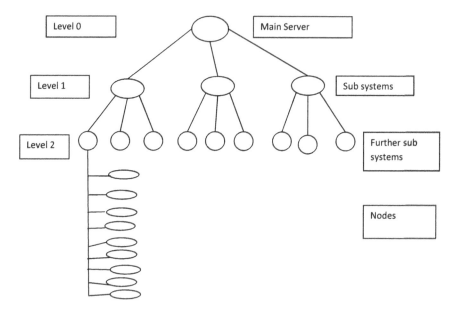

Fig 3.1: hierarchy of scheduling

As shown in figure here processer from LEVEL 2 will request for job to processer at LEVEL 1 and FROM LEVEL 1 it will request to LEVEL 0. Now main server at LEVEL 0 will assign job to processer at LEVEL 1 and LEVEL 1 processor will further distribute process. Now all jobs were assigning and at LEVEL 2 it will distribute jobs to further processers to execute. Here we were going to assign 200 chunks of files as job to test performance.

28

Design of Methodology:

Fig 3.2: Implementation Design

Further it can be distributed according to BPU speed on the different nodes.

All the processors in the systems find their BPU request according to the total sum of their BPUs range. In the system all the processors perform the task divide equally on the processors.

At time when all the jobs equally divide on the processors apply the round robin for execution of the processor this method to find the waiting time and response time of the job.

In the adaptive hierarchical scheduling policy assign the job assignment, affinity scheduling and self scheduling approach in unified framework to assign resources to parallel jobs. It is achieved by the exploring the parent child relationship between the nodes in the cluster tree.

29

3.4 Algorithm:

If state (unbiased) = 1 then

If top level = 1

If (queue task) = ^ then

Send back the request (task)

Else

      Execute the task

End if

End if (Top level is ≠ 1 and outer node is ≠ 1) then

If (Next (table) = ^) then if

If (Next (TTR) = ^) then if

Send TTR to parent node

End if

Send back the task

Else

Execute the task

End if

Else

Send task request to the parent level

End if

End if

Here TTR is task transfer request.

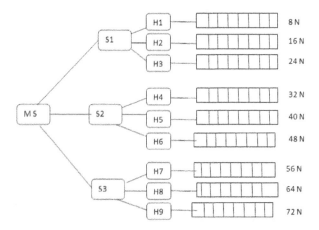

Figure3.3: Tree approach defined in system

Time sharing approach helps to balance the load in number of jobs on process nodes and also helps to allocate that job to nodes can execute according to its capacity which results in getting less weight time for the jobs. After this the time sharing technique execute jobs which are allocated jobs according to job sharing techniques and result in producing less response time then the existing systems. The space sharing technique also allows splitting the job on different processing nodes if one node is not able to full the requirements of the job then the job will be split on the different processing nodes which makes job to be executed in less time. The proposed system also uses the demand driven approach to make the results of the system more efficient. In the demand driven approach if the node is in idle state then he will demand its parent for the jobs and if the parent does not have the job then he will demand the job from his parent will makes the system to wait less for the jobs. In the work load model all tasks of jobs have equal service demand. Job cumulative service demand is dividing into maximum jobs and each job will have a demand of minimum time. This work load shows the advantage of space sharing policy. The adaptive scheduling used for Heterogeneous Multi-cluster System can be framed using following steps:

I) **Job selection:** Job selection policy is used to select the jobs in the queue. The global scheduler consist the jobs in the queue. The aim of scheduling policy is to carry the job from the queue in some manner. So we use First Come First Serve policy. It is one of the simple policies and it has less overhead as compare to other policies. It

31

implements just one queue which holds the tasks in order they come in. The job is served in arrival order.

II) **Selecting site**: The Site/Cluster is selected on which the job runs. The Most-fit policy is used to select the cluster. The perfect policy is used to minimize the data that is divided into fragments by choosing the appropriate cluster which waste less number of processing nodes and by taking care of the other jobs in the queue.

- In the scenario we define the tree structure in which main system divide into three main systems. After these three main system divide into further three nodes, it contain total 9 hosts in the system. Each node connected with 8 processing nodes.

- All the nodes find their BPU request according to the total sum of their BPUs range. In the system all the processing nodes perform the task divide equally on the processors.

- At time when all the jobs equally divide on the processors apply the round robin for execution of the processor this method to find the waiting time and when the job get executed.

- In the first step define the tree structure in which main system divide into three main systems. After these three main system divide into further three nodes, it contain total 9 nodes in the system. Each node connected with 8 processors.

And after all scheduling and allocation of chunks it will be stored in the file allocation table by means of the parameters such as BPU, starting time, ending time, node id .at each and every iterations this file table will be updated so that if a hacker come to attack a piece of file also it is highly impossible to integrate all parts of files because its locations are frequently updated and allocation table will also acts dynamically in order to make the complexity level in security

CHAPTER 4 - RESULT AND DISCUSSIONS

Results and Discusions:

1. There is a single system scheduler which is at top and act as global name node. All jobs are submitted here exponentially for which we have to create traces.

2. Our architecture is 4 levels deep. At last level we have 72 processing nodes N_1 to N_{72} (each cluster have 8 nodes in it and there are 9 clusters H_1 to H_8 in total so $9*8 = 72$)

3. In figure: 3.3 have shown cluster H_5 with 8 processing nodes N_{33} to N_{40}.

4. Each node is having its local queue for storing jobs for time sharing purpose.

5. Every processing node in a cluster consists of different number of BPUs (Intra cluster heterogeneity). Number of BPUs for each processor is fixed. For example N_{33} = 1 BPU, N_{34} = 4 BPUs, N_{35} = 2 BPUs, N_{36} = 12 BPUs, N_{37} = 2 BPUs, N_{38} = 3 BPUs, N_{39} = 10 BPUs, N_{40} = 7 BPUs.

6. In starting System is in neutral state. There are no jobs in intermediate layers or with processors. Jobs travel down the hierarchy based on the demand from the processing nodes.

7. Multiprogramming Level (MPL) of all the processor is also fixed. We have formula to calculate MPL of each processor. MPL=(Processor speed ×Basic MPL)/(slowest processor speed). Or we can make it fixed (preferred) to simplify it. We can fix it to 2 i.e. each processing nodes can do time-sharing between two jobs. For time-sharing we use Round Robin algorithm.

Define the request ID for the entire job those present in the main server with name. In the form of input give the arrival time capacity to the system with according to their range.

Request	SystemName	StartTime	EndTime	Capacity
1	virtual host 1	0.249387	12.871570	10
42	virtual host 1	8.209470	0.167761	7
61	virtual host 1	13.939573	8.782249	8
102	virtual host 1	23.090017	0.448630	5
121	virtual host 1	29.259983	2.032285	4
151	virtual host 1	46.433290	1.065963	2
192	virtual host 1	51.222079	0.674594	6
3	virtual host 2	1.600055	1.352049	37
6	virtual host 2	2.322231	8.379447	41

Fig4.1: All the value allocated from main server

All the values further pass to the sub virtual host level where define the start and end time for every server that is connected with main server. All the servers find their request according to the total sum of their capacity range. In the system all the resources perform the task divide equally on the processors.

Request	System	StartTime	Node	EndTime	Capacity
1	virtual host 1	0.249387	sub virtual host 2	12.871570	10
42	virtual host 1	8.209470	sub virtual host 2	0.167761	7
61	virtual host 1	13.939573	sub virtual host 2	8.782249	8
102	virtual host 1	23.090017	sub virtual host 2	0.448630	5
121	virtual host 1	29.259983	sub virtual host 2	2.032285	4
151	virtual host 1	46.433290	sub virtual host 2	1.065963	2
192	virtual host 1	51.222079	sub virtual host 2	0.674594	6
3	virtual host 2	1.600055	sub virtual host 4	1.352049	37
6	virtual host 2	2.322231	sub virtual host 5	8.379447	41
9	virtual host 2	2.623456	sub virtual host 6	9.025692	56
11	virtual host 2	3.438491	sub virtual host 4	0.852009	29
12	virtual host 2	3.461531	sub virtual host 4	1.189170	3
14	virtual host 2	3.658235	sub virtual host 4	7.258019	32
15	virtual host 2	3.755783	sub virtual host 4	5.034758	12
17	virtual host 2	4.284211	sub virtual host 5	16.992225	42
18	virtual host 2	4.327209	sub virtual host 4	2.219272	26

Fig 4.2: Pass all values to sub host that connected with the server 1, 2 and 3

At time when all the resources equally divide on the sub virtual host apply the round robin for execution of the processor this method to find the waiting time and response time of the request. In the policy use the round robin policy to assign the job on the different sub virtual hosts to the schedule the all resources in equal time.

Request	System	StartTime	Node	EndTime	Capac
2	virtual host 3	1.573859	sub virtual host 8	68.359852	60
3	virtual host 2	1.600055	sub virtual host 4	1.352049	37
4	virtual host 3	1.698999	sub virtual host 8	5.106801	3
52	virtual host 2	10.501433	sub virtual host 4	31.493595	34
53	virtual host 2	10.554602	sub virtual host 4	2.744210	1
54	virtual host 3	10.673146	sub virtual host 8	6.118381	64
55	virtual host 2	13.160303	sub virtual host 5	128.369386	43
56	virtual host 2	13.225586	sub virtual host 4	3.369462	17
57	virtual host 3	13.635781	sub virtual host 7	21.171335	72
58	virtual host 2	13.654674	sub virtual host 6	0.975126	51
59	virtual host 2	13.746298	sub virtual host 4	4.729004	23
61	virtual host 1	13.939573	sub virtual host 2	8.782249	8
62	virtual host 3	14.012369	sub virtual host 8	3.757238	64
63	virtual host 2	14.022246	sub virtual host 4	0.509777	31
64	virtual host 3	14.059885	sub virtual host 8	1.942654	11
65	virtual host 3	14.264492	sub virtual host 7	10.560373	68
66	virtual host 2	14.441173	sub virtual host 5	9.119042	47
67	virtual host 3	14.509571	sub virtual host 8	3.530198	15
68	virtual host 3	14.642158	sub virtual host 9	6.843209	83
69	virtual host 3	14.716038	sub virtual host 6	3.813171	50
70	virtual host 3	15.207249	sub virtual host 8	25.352803	23
71	virtual host 2	15.208342	sub virtual host 4	0.056402	33
72	virtual host 2	16.407854	sub virtual host 4	61.910291	8
73	virtual host 3	16.561286	sub virtual host 8	7.919094	58
74	virtual host 2	16.704214	sub virtual host 5	7.376917	40
75	virtual host 2	16.707016	sub virtual host 4	0.144641	16
76	virtual host 3	16.936171	sub virtual host 7	11.827332	74

Fig4.3: Start time end time of the resources

36

Waiting queue and completed process time utilized

Average Response Time 00:45:53.8528273   Average Waiting Time 00:45:40.871978

EndTime	Capacity	WaitingQueue	CompletedProcess	SubResou
3 68.359852	60	00:00:26.6867332	00:00:26.8164018	P57
4 1.352049	37	00:00:01.6203956	00:00:01.6593702	P25
3 5.106801	3	00:00:23.9621702	00:00:23.9621904	P63
4 31.493595	34	00:00:01.3264758	00:00:01.3265029	P30
4 2.744210	1	00:00:00.0138803	00:00:00.0138977	P32
3 6.118381	64	00:00:28.9763367	00:00:29.1243151	P58
5 128.369386	43	00:00:03.2738626	00:00:03.2738816	P33
4 3.369462	17	00:00:00.4118267	00:00:00.4257924	P25
7 21.171335	72	00:00:18.4071290	00:00:18.4071565	P53
5 0.975126	51	00:00:07.3038123	00:00:07.3705662	P45
4 4.729004	23	00:00:00.5390581	00:00:00.5568194	P25
2 8.782249	8	00:00:00.1943197	00:00:00.1943371	P12
3 3.757238	64	00:00:28.9781290	00:00:29.1270763	P57
4 0.509777	31	00:00:00.8854473	00:00:00.9148421	P28
3 1.942654	11	00:00:23.9778015	00:00:23.9778245	P61
7 10.560373	68	00:00:14.9111167	00:00:14.9946588	P49
5 9.119042	47	00:00:05.0661628	00:00:05.1251989	P33
3 3.530198	15	00:00:23.0418415	00:00:23.1466341	P58
9 6.843209	83	00:00:41.6225774	00:00:41.7916649	P69
5 3.813171	50	00:00:06.4808030	00:00:06.5447642	P41
3 25.352803	23	00:00:24.8383487	00:00:24.9517705	P57
4 0.056402	33	00:00:01.0593741	00:00:01.0916042	P28
4 61.910291	8	00:00:00.0189317	00:00:00.0189438	P25
3 7.919094	58	00:00:26.1453024	00:00:26.2708098	P58
5 7.376917	40	00:00:02.2064727	00:00:02.2502475	P33
4 0.144641	16	00:00:00.3154721	00:00:00.3266750	P25
7 11.827332	74	00:00:19.7576920	00:00:19.8531464	P49

Fig 4.4: Waiting queue completed process of the job

Graphical Representation:

Main system divides the resources

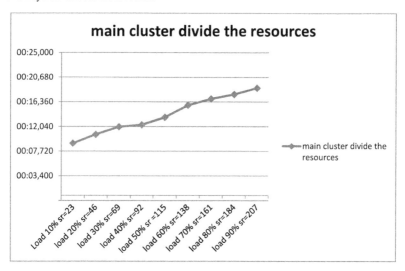

Fig 4.5: Main systems divide the resources on the other servers.

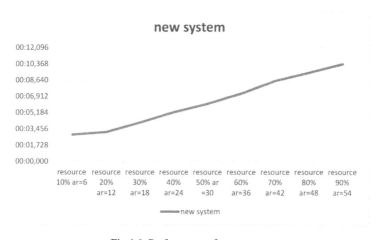

Fig 4.6: Performance of our system

38

Tabular representation

resources	Average wait time new system	Average Waiting time old system
resources10% ar=6	00:02.840	00:03.117
	00:03.112	00:03.384
resources 20% ar=12	00:04.123	00:04.856
resources30% ar=18	00:05.224	00:05.999
	00:06.111	00:06.455
resources 40% ar=24	00:07.222	00:07.888
resources50% ar=30	00:08.567	00:09.111
	00:09.445	00:10.111
resources 60% ar=36	00:10.345	00:11.234
resources70% ar=42		
resources 80% ar=48		
resources 90% ar=54		

Fig 4.7: Tabular representation

Graphical Representation:

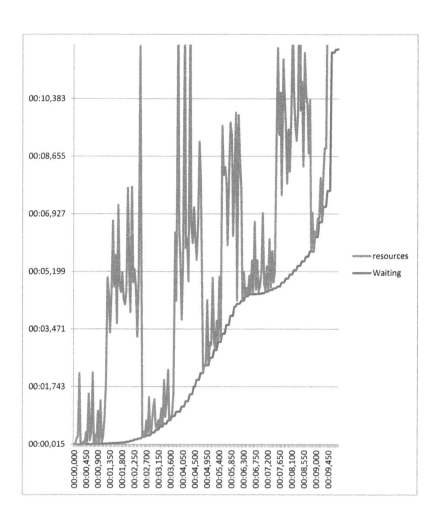

Fig 4.8: graphical representation

CHAPTER 5 - CONCLUSTION AND FUTURE SCOPE

5.1 Conclusion

In this dissertation work, a new scalable and efficient scheduling algorithm in distributed file system is planned and then enforced in virtual cloud computing environment using Microsoft visual studio, in c# language. Our proposal is to balance the loads of nodes, to increase the processing speed in file system and also to reduce the cost as much as possible. This thesis presents design of a scalable and efficient distributed file system. The system uses a light weight front and back end server to manage sessions and compute the storage and processing of data. This design solves the potential bottleneck scenario that the name node server of current systems by can be allocation the work load into further host. Our research work conjointly offers an adaptive and efficient resource allocation scheme which may lead to full link utilization and hence much reduced chunk transfer time. By visualizing the parameters in graphs and tables we can able to simply identify that the response time and data centre processing time is improved yet as well as cost is reduced in comparison to the existing scheduling parameters. Based on the numerical results presented, our algorithm will overcome standard existing distributed file systems .our model can be directly implemented in current distributed file systems.

5.2 Future Scope

The future work includes overcoming the problem of deadlocks and server overflow. The potency and effectiveness of our design are additional validated by analytical models and a real implementation with a small-scale environment by passing real world data to store and process. At present functioning on a lot of elaborate experiments to implement our system and test it in real cloud computing environment.

CHAPTER 6 - REFERENCES

[1] Lee, D. Patterson, A. Rabkin, I. Stoica, and M. Zaharia. (2009, Feb. 10)," *Above the clouds: A Berkeley view of cloud computing"*, EECS Dept., Univ. California, Berkeley, No. UCB/EECS-2009-28.

[2] Martin Randles, Enas Odat, David Lamb, Osama Abu- Rahmeh and A. Taleb-Bendiab, "A Comparative Experiment in Distributed Load Balancing", 2009 Second International Conference on Developments in eSystems Engineering.

[3] Ali M. Alakeel, (2010), *"A Guide to Dynamic Load Balancing in Distributed Computer Systems"*,International Journal of Computer Science and Network Security, VOL.10 No.6, June 2010.

[4] Amandeep Kaur Sidhu, Supriya Kinger,(2013)," *Analysis of Load Balancing Techniques in Cloud Computing"*, International Journal of Computers & Technology,Volume 4 No. 2.

[5] Debessay Fesehaye, Rahul Malik, Klara Nahrstedt, A Scalable Distributed File System for Cloud Computing.(n.d)[online]. Available: http://citeseerx.ist.psu.edu/viewdoc/download?doi=10.1.1.176.5236&rep=rep1&type=pdf

[6] Cloud computing principles, systems and applications NICK Antonopoulos (n.d.)[online]. Available : http://mgitech.wordpress.com.

[7] Anthony T.Velte, Toby J.Velte, Robert Elsenpeter,*"Cloud Computing A Practical Approach"*, TATA McGRAW-HILL Edition 2010.

[8] Mladen A. Vouk, Cloud Computing Issues, Research and Implementations, Proceedings of the ITI 2008 30th International Conference on Information Technology Interfaces, 2008, June 23-26.

[9] lizhe wang, rajiv Ranjan. (n.d.). Cloud Computing Methodology, Systems and Applications. Available:http://www.unitiv.com.

[10] Luyang Dong, Bin Gong, (2012), *"A Hierarchical Scheduling Policy for Large-Scale Rendering"*,IEEE International Conference on Systems, Man, and Cybernetics, 2012.

[11] Tejinder Sharma, Vijay Kumar Banga, (2013), *"Efficient and Enhanced Algorithm in Cloud Computing"*, International Journal of Soft Computing and Engineering (IJSCE) ISSN: 2231-2307, Volume-3, Issue-1.

[12] Jasmin James, Dr. Bhupendra Verma,(2012)," *Efficient VM Load Balancing Algorithm For A Cloud Computing Environment"*, Jasmin James et al. International Journal on Computer Science and Engineering (IJCSE),Vol-4,Issue No.9.

[13] J. H. Abawajy and S. P. Dandamudi, *"Parallel job scheduling on multicluster computing systems,"* in Proceedings of the IEEE International Conference on Cluster Computing,Hong Kong, China, 2003, pp. 11-18.

[14] Jaliya Ekanayake and Geoffrey Fox, High Performance Parallel Computing with Clouds and Cloud Technologies, Presented at Cloud Computing - First International Conference, CloudComp, Munich, Germany,2009

[15] Jonthan Strickland. How Cloud Computing Works(n.d.) [online]. Available:http://www.howstuffworks.com/cloud-computing/cloud-computing1.html

[16] Abhisek Pan, John Paul Walters, Vijay S. Pai, Dong-In D. Kang, Stephen P. Crago, "Integrating High Performance File Systems in a Cloud Computing Environment", The International Workshop on Data-Intensive Scalable Computing Systems (DISCS), in conjunction with the 2012 ACM/IEEE Supercomputing Conference (SC'12), November 2012.

[17] Hung-Chang Hsiao, Member, Hsueh-Yi Chung, Haiying Shen,, and Yu-Chang Chao,(2013)," *Load Rebalancing for Distributed File Systems in Clouds"*, IEEE Transactions On Parallel And Distributed Systems, Vol. 24, No. 5.

[18] Cong Wang, Qian Wang, and Kui Ren, Wenjing Lou, Privacy-Preserving Public Auditing for Data Storage Security in Cloud Computing, Presented at IEEE INFOCOM 2010.

[19] Satoshi Togawa, Kazuhide Kanenishi, Private Cloud Cooperation Framework of e-Learning Environment for Disaster Recovery , IEEE International Conference on Systems, Man, and Cybernetics, 2013.

[22] Sabrina Zimara,(2013,Jul.12). The Five Essential Characteristics of Cloud Computing. Available: http://erpbloggers.com/2013/07/the-five-essential-characteristics-of-cloud-computing/#sthash.DqMVgsD0.dpuf.

[21] Sonal Guleria1, Dr. Sonia Vatta2, (2013)"To Enhance Multimedia Security In Cloud Computing Environment Using Crossbreed Algorithm",International Journal of Application or Innovation in Engineering and Management, Volume 2, Issue 6.

[22] CemOzdogan,(2011, Feb.14). Round robin scheduling.[online]. Available: http://siber.cankaya.edu.tr/OperatingSystems/ceng328/node125.html.

[23] John Grady, 2014, 7 Major Current Trends in Cloud Computing , [online]. Available: http://www.circleid.com/posts/20140303_7_major_current_trends_in_cloud_com puting/

[24] CloudTweaks (n.d.)[online]. Available:http://cloudtweaks.com/2012/09/key-features-of-cloud-computing/.

[25] http://javahungry.blogspot.com/2013/09/round-robin-scheduling-algorithm-with-example-java-program-code.html.

- Intstallation step of visual studio 2010

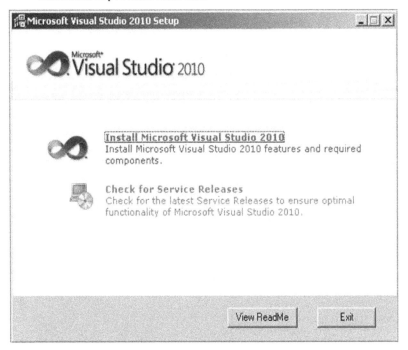

- Enter the key in the visual studio

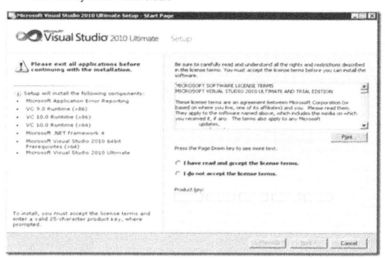

- Install all packages of different platforms

46

- Installation of SQL Server installation

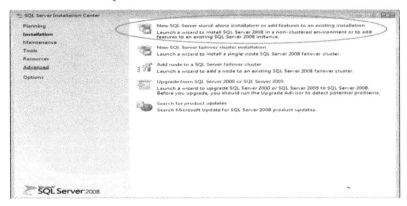

- Pass all parameter before install completion

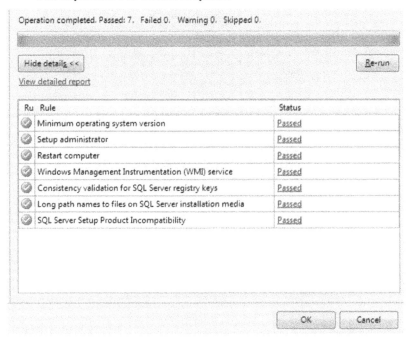

- Select all the features from sql setup

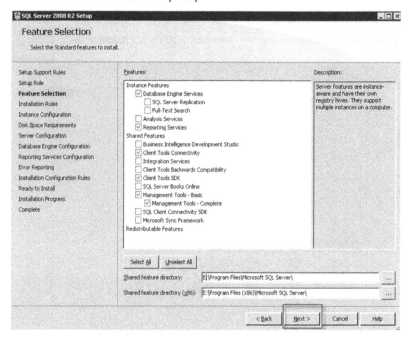

- Starting screen of the SQL server

- Go for new project and start doing coding in visual studio 2010

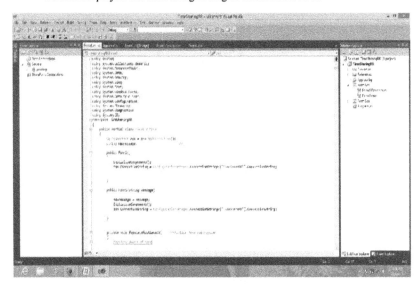

- Launch SQL server management and connect back end of our project

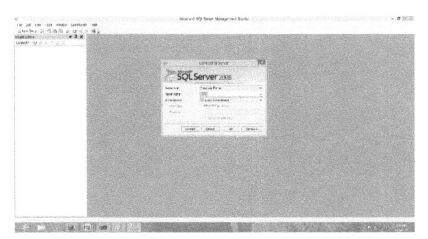

- Execute the code from visual studio 2010

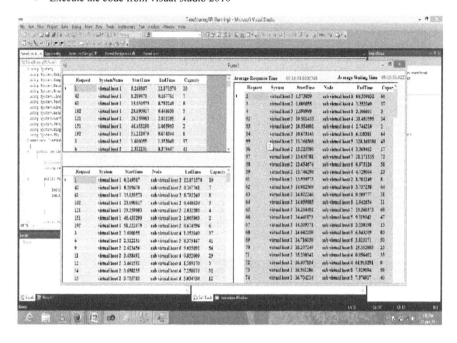

List of Abbreviations

BYOD	Bring Your Own Device
CIA	Confidentiality, Integrity & Availability
CPU	Central Processing Unit
FIFO	First In First Out
GFS	Google File System
HDFS	Hadoop Distributed File System
HPC	High Performance Computing
IaaS	Infrastructure-as-a-Service
MD	Message Digest
MFS	Mirror File System
PaaS	Platform-as-a-Service
PC	Personal Computer
RR	Round Robin
TCP	Transmission Control Protocol
TPA	Third Party Auditor
VM	Virtual Machine